DATE DUE

The Political Thought of Sir Henry Vane the Younger

PUBLICATIONS IN THE HANEY FOUNDATION SERIES

The Political Thought
of
Sir Henry Vane

the *Younger*

MARGARET A. JUDSON

UNIVERSITY OF PENNSYLVANIA PRESS

PHILADELPHIA

*Publication of this book has been made possible by a grant
from the Haney Foundation of the University of Pennsylvania*

Library of Congress Catalog Card Number: 75-83138

SBN: 8122-7599-3

Printed in the United States of America

Preface

This short study of the political thought of Sir Henry Vane the Younger grew out of the research I began in 1954 on the political ideas in the period of the Commonwealth and Protectorate in England. In my investigations I came to realize that Vane was a political thinker of more stature than to date has been recognized.

The primary purpose of this essay is to present and interpret Vane as a political thinker. It is also my hope that an understanding of his political ideas and their significance for him will illuminate some aspects of his career which continue to perplex historians.

I should like to express my appreciation to the Guggenheim Foundation and to the Rutgers Research Council for their help which made possible the research for this essay and to the Haney Foundation of the University of Pennsylvania for their assistance in its publication.

M. A. J.

Highland Park, New Jersey
May 1969

*The Political Thought of Sir Henry Vane
the Younger*

Early Political Ideas

Between 1640 and 1660 in England, writers set forth in Parliament, pulpit, and press such varied and challenging political ideas that scholars are still amazed at the wealth of political thought emerging from these critical years. Almost each year a new book, presenting a fresh interpretation of Hobbes or the Levellers appears. Harrington is still studied as one of the "founding fathers" of the American constitution. Filmer, Parker, Winstanley, and others are now recognized as political thinkers who made significant contributions to the battle of ideas waged during this revolutionary period.

This essay will focus attention on the political ideas of another theorist at this time, Sir Henry Vane the Younger. His concept of the necessity of the separation of government and religion, his vision of right government as a true association of consenting individuals, his concern for the superiority of civil over military authority, and his ideas of obedience in civil society mark him as a political thinker worthy of more serious consideration than has hitherto been accorded him.

Unlike his contemporary theorists Hobbes, Harrington, the Levellers, and others, Vane spent much of his adult life actually participating at a high level in the councils of government. Governor of Massachusetts in 1636, when he was only twenty-three years old, a leading member of the Long Parliament from 1640 until its dissolution in 1653, treasurer of the navy from 1642 to 1650, active member of every council of state in the Commonwealth from 1649 to 1653, close friend and eventually bitter enemy of Cromwell, a leader in the Republic in 1659, Vane stands out as one of the three or four most important men in the Puritan Revolution. His stature was clearly recognized by Charles II and his advisors in 1660 after the Restoration. Although Vane was no regicide, as he correctly and stoutly maintained at his trial, the new government regarded him as so radical and dangerous an opponent of monarchy that he was imprisoned, tried, and executed in 1662.

During all his career Vane was a figure almost as controversial to his contemporaries as Cromwell. Modern historians have been baffled by him and have not yet assessed and portrayed adequately the part he played in English history between 1640 and 1660. With the current interest in the period and the sources and approaches now available for studying it, a full-scale biography of Vane is long overdue.[1]

Although there will be no attempt in this short essay, concerned primarily with his political ideas, to deal with his career as such, an understanding of

Vane's political ideas sheds light on some of the controversial dark spots of his career. In the last years of his life, particularly in *The People's Case* and in the material prepared for his trial, Vane gave, in retrospect, an explanation of the earlier ideas which had influenced his political behavior. A discussion of his later interpretation of himself will appear at the end of this essay.[2]

If his political career has not received the treatment it merits, his political ideas have been neglected even more. They have been dismissed too casually or misunderstood, perhaps because Vane buried some of his most fundamental political thought in a work concerned primarily with his mystical religious views. Also some of his other important ideas are found in an obscure short pamphlet written in answer to Harrington. Vane pondered long and hard upon the ageless problems of man, God, and society and enunciated political theories which, in the penetration of the questions raised and the quality of the answers given, compare remarkably well with the theories of other better-known thinkers in this illustrious age.

Until 1655 Vane's political ideas were set forth in fragmentary form in his speeches and letters and not in formal tracts or treatises. These clearly indicate that early in life Vane had developed ideas which helped to influence his actions. As an introduction to his more mature political theory, the most significant of those earlier beliefs will first be briefly presented, using only his own statements made at the time and not his own later justification of his views and actions.

In 1637, Vane almost prophetically set forth ideas to which, under one circumstance or another, he held fast throughout the rest of his life. In a controversy in Massachusetts between Winthrop and Vane over a new law which threatened to refuse admission to the colony to persons regarded as dangerous Antinomians, Vane took the stand that every man was a child of God. Neither a Christian church nor a Christian commonwealth had the right, he maintained, to refuse admission to a child of God. Government had no rightful authority over the spirit of man which was God-given.[3] "That law which gives that without limitation to man, which is proper to God, cannot be just."[4] ". . . whatsoever is done by word or deed, in church or commonwealth, must be done in the name of the Lord Jesus."[5] "Now if you will define a Christian common-wealth there must be put in, such a consent as is according to God: a subjecting to such a government as is according unto Christ."[6] No government, whether in church or state, could be a right government, one according to God's law and Christian principles, if it did not allow and respect the spiritual freedom of each individual. All

his life Vane maintained this belief in spiritual freedom from governmental control. Yet even in the statement from which the previous quotations have been
taken, Vane revealed that he was not a mere vision-
ary or utopian, but a man who possessed a knowledge of the law of England and the position of the
king in her government. For the magistrates in
Massachusetts Bay to exclude Christians took away,
Vane argued, the king's right of "planting some of
his subjects amongst us."[7]

In 1641 Vane, who had returned to England, became a spokesman for the group in the Long Parliament working for the abolition of episcopacy "root
and branch." Episcopal government, he insisted, led
to "a spirit of pride, exalting itself above its fellow
Presbyterians under the power of a Bishop, then
over its fellow Bishops under the title of Arch-
bishops."[8] Such a government, with its tyranny over
the spirits of men, all of whom are children of God,
was not of God's choosing and must be uprooted.
Episcopacy was "a great impediment to the perfect
reformation and growth of religion, and very preju-
dicial to the civil state."[9] ". . . if we do not at this
time pull down this government, we are seeming 'to
check' Divine Providence." "For hath not this Parliament been called, continued, preserved and se-
cured, by the immediate finger of God, as it were for
this work?" The root and branch bill must be passed

"to glorify God," and to "comply with His Providence."[10]

In the succeeding years, up to the death of the king in 1649, Vane worked, as is well known, for liberty of conscience. He feared Scotch presbyterianism perhaps as much as Anglican episcopacy, because it, too, could so easily tyrannize over the spirit of individual men. Vane is generally regarded as responsible for the inclusion, in the Solemn League and Covenant, of the phrase, "according to the word of God," which may mean freedom of conscience.[11] In the heated debates taking place over religion in 1644 between the English and Scotch, Vane, according to Baillie, "reasoned for a full liberty of conscience to all religions without any exceptions."[12] As late as 1648 Vane "did his best to persuade Charles . . . to accept the scheme of toleration, set forth in the Heads of Proposals."[13] He was convinced that no government, whether of church or state, was right, i.e., in accord with God's plan, if it denied freedom of conscience to individual men who were children of God.

In the years between 1641 and 1649 Vane was an ardent and active leader, working for greater Parliamentary power. He supported the laws passed in the early months of the Long Parliament limiting the king's power and increasing the power of Parliament. He was the young man who furnished the fateful evidence employed so skillfully by Pym against Strafford in 1641. It is possible that Vane helped to write the first part of the Grand Remonstrance.[14] After the death of Pym, he stood out as one of several leaders of the War Party in Parliament which worked to push the war through to a decisive military victory. Nevertheless, in the negotiations between 1646 and 1648 involving the king, the Scotch, Parliament, and the army, Vane was willing to continue a form of government which allowed for a king, though with greatly reduced power. In September, 1647, according to Firth, he "opposed Marten's motion that no further application should be made to the king" and again in January, 1648, took the same stand. In April, 1648, he voted with those declaring that "they would not alter 'the fundamental government of the kingdom by king, lords, and commons.' " In September, 1648, Vane was one of the commissioners at Newport who still, after the second Civil War, argued for an agreement with the king if it included religious toleration.[15]

Since, however, no satisfactory terms could be reached with Charles, Vane finally came to the conclusion that civil government should be and could be set up without the king. He explained to the Commons that the king "still reserved a power in himself, or at least to his posterity, to exercise as tyrannical a government as he had formerly done."[16]

With internal and foreign enemies subdued, Vane told the Commons, "there was nothing wanting but their own consent and resolution to make themselves the happiest nation and people in the world."[17] God had done His part and now it was up to man to do his. Yet Vane refused, as he steadfastly explained at his own trial in 1662, to accept Pride's Purge or to take part in the proceedings of the king's trial. Why he took such a stand has never been satisfactorily explained, but a study of his political principles, later formulated, does shed light on his actions at this critical time.[18]

After the execution of the king, Vane refused to take the first engagement or oath in which approval of the trial and execution of the king was required for members of the Council of State. Apparently he took the second engagement of February, 1649, which required only his acceptance of the setting up of a republic without king or House of Lords.[19] During the four years of the Commonwealth, Vane continued to be one of the two or three most important members of the councils of state and of the Commons.[20] As treasurer of the Navy until late in 1650, as member of the Admiralty Committee, and as one of the extraordinary commissioners for the fleet, he proved to be a successful administrator. In the struggle of power politics which the government of the new commonwealth was playing to defeat its enemies

and win recognition and support from other coun-
tries, Vane played a skillful game—one praised by
two contemporaries, Milton and Sykes, Vane's friend
and first biographer. It was Vane, Milton wrote in
his sonnet, who could discern

> The drift of hollow states, hard to be spelled;
> Then to advise how wars may best upheld,
> Move by her two main nerves, iron and gold.[21]

According to Sykes, Vane could "conjecture and spell
out the most reserved consults and secret drifts of
foreign councils against us (which they reckoned as
tacita concealed till executed), the Hollander did
experience to their cost."[22]

Even Vane himself, who refers often to his own
high principles and concern for the public welfare,
wanted Cromwell to recognize that his navy [i.e.,
Vane's] as well as Cromwell's army played a part in
the victories God had given England. God "hath de-
lighted," he wrote Cromwell, "as much visibly to
take the glory to Himself in all this last year's enter-
prise by sea, as well as by land."[23] And again he wrote
to Thomas Scott, "so that you may be sensible how
the Lord makes His goodness and mercy to this
Commonwealth sound forth in the South, as well
as in the North."[24]

If Vane took satisfaction in God's stamp of approval upon his conduct of naval affairs, he was far
from satisfied with the main task he believed God

had called Englishmen to perform. God had given them the opportunity to establish a true commonwealth based on right principles and they had not risen to the task. Vane wrote in 1651, ". . . we are like the children of Israel in former times, rather hardened and made worse, for the most of us, by God's appearances and deliverances than brought nearer to Him, which if it continues with us, will be bitterness in the latter end."[25] Vane was impatient that while God stood aside and waited, men in power "contest and babble," which, he says, "of all things are most grievous to me." These men "will not suffer to be done things that are so plain as that they ought to do themselves."[26] He was fully aware, he told Cromwell, that when Cromwell with God's help subdued Scotland, there would be "greater trials and difficulties than ever about the right way of settling that, which by such a constant series of successes hath been obtained, for which changes the Lord fit us, and continue your lordship an instrument in His hand, to serve Him in your *generation* to the praise of His grace and good of His people."[27] By 1653 Vane and Cromwell came to differ sharply on the method for arranging the election of a new Parliament. When in April, 1653, Cromwell dissolved the Rump and chastised Vane, he interrupted the public career of this eminent statesman for more than five years.

Like Machiavelli, Vane retired from public life and like Machiavelli turned to writing. What were the problems with which he struggled in his retirement? We can only conjecture, but drawing upon both his previous experiences and ideas and also upon the writings he produced between 1655 and his execution in 1662, we might reconstruct his soul searching.[28] God had given man a remarkable opportunity in those years and man had failed to do his part. The "ecclesiastical tyranny" of Laud and also of the Presbyterians had been ended, but the result was a far cry from the true religious freedom he had sought since his youth. New men coming into power were tempted to use "worldly government" for their own glory, rather than God's, thereby erecting new spiritual tyrannies. Was it possible, Vane must have queried, for true spiritual freedom ever to be realized? Moreover, although the tyranny of the king's arbitrary power had been ended, there was increasing danger that a new arbitrary power, that of military might, might take full control over Parliament and Englishmen's destinies. Would it ever be possible for the people to whom God had given this great opportunity to rule themselves rightly? If Parliament should succeed in controlling the military, would its members ever learn to control themselves and cease "contesting and babbling" among themselves? Members of Parliament were using their position of trust for their own private interests and not for the public welfare. It must have become clear to him that the evils of self-interested arbitrary government had not ended when the king was dead. New men in positions of power showed themselves liable to the same temptations. Any government, whether of king or Parliament, bishop or Puritan saint, could become tyrannical.

Until the dissolution of the Long Parliament in 1653, Vane's long and distinguished career had been marked by his active participation in the great controversies of the time, first in Massachusetts and then in England. Early in his life he had formulated certain religious and political beliefs which had provided guidelines for his actions, but it was not until his retirement in 1653 that Vane became a true political philosopher. In this role he drew not only upon his earlier ideas but also upon his realization that men had failed to establish true freedom and right government after 1649. The failures of those years of the Commonwealth could not be blamed just upon a king or upon bishops or presbyters. Englishmen themselves who took over the government had acted tyrannically.

His grasp of this truth must have led to a fundamental inner struggle. Were his earlier ideals impossible of human realization, as his experiences in the years particularly from 1649 to 1653 seemed to indicate? Should he give up the struggle to achieve spiritual freedom for all and right government for England? With his mystical leanings should he become concerned only with his own individual soul and salvation? Because of his intense religious faith, this course of action might have been an easy one. Or, should he continue to be interested in government, shaping his views concerning it on the stark political realities he had observed, thus divorcing his views of man's spiritual nature from his ideas of man's political organization and behavior? Strange as it may seem, this course might have been possible for Vane to follow. It has already been suggested that he was a cool and discerning politician as well as an idealist. Later, in 1659, he showed that he grasped more clearly than Cromwell had, England's true interest in the power struggle between France and Spain going on in Europe.[29] Might not Vane have been tempted to view all government as realistically as he viewed foreign affairs and become a Puritan Machiavelli? The historian can only speculate over the different roles which he considered, for Vane himself does not give us direct evidence concerning his inner struggle. We do know, however, that in his writings following 1653 he re-examined and reaffirmed his basic beliefs and in so doing became a true political philosopher, raising such profound questions and giving such reasoned answers that he merits a high place among the English political philosophers of this creative age.

The Mature Political Thinker

In *The Retired Man's Meditations or the Mystery and Power of Godliness* (1655)[30] Vane first set forth his more profound political ideas. In 1656 there appeared *A Healing Question propounded and resolved upon Occasion of the late Call to Humiliation*.[31] Next came *A Needful Corrective or Ballance in Popular Government expressed in a Letter to James Harrington, Esquire, upon occasion of a late Treatise of his*.[32] *The People's Case Stated* was probably written when he was in prison, sometime between 1660 and 1662.[33] Statements he made in his trial or prepared for it were printed in 1662.[34] The remarks and speeches of Vane, made in Parliament in 1659 and reported in Burton's Diary[35] are also an invaluable source for his political ideas. In addition, there are several short tracts dealing with political ideas, attributed to Vane and bound together with the British Museum copy of *The People's Case Stated*.[36] The ideas expressed in these tracts indicate Vane's authorship. The full stature of Vane as a political theorist can best be recognized by discussing his work as a whole, not by examining each work separately. Moreover, there was no important change in his ideas once they had been enunciated in *The Retired Man's Meditations,* although some aspects of his thought are set forth only in his later writings.

In these more formal writings produced between 1655 and 1662 Vane remained true to his earlier belief that each man was a child of God, created by Him in His own image and possessing within himself, by God's grace and Christ's redemption, the capacity to behave and think as God's child. Men were, he explained in *The Retired Man's Meditations*

> ... the candle and lamp of the Lord, that is fed with oil out of the holy candlestick from Christ . . . enabling them to a discerning of good and evil, according to the light and principles of that natural righteousness wherein they were at first created; and requiring them to exercise and improve this talent and ability of mind, freely given unto them . . .[37]

Vane stressed the potential of all men, pointing out that "there is no man that comes into the world, wherever he be born or educated, but is in a capacity of being respected by God, as a natural righteous man."[38] He also recognized that men are essentially equal: ". . . men in their creation and births are made of one blood, all the nations of them, Acts 17:26, and so are equal, and cannot therefore be distinguished and fixed in such different conditions and capabilities of rulers and subjects."[39] For man to rule man, his spiritual brother, had long created a problem for Vane, and it was this problem which became central in his more fully developed political thought.

Vane recognized that individual man faced obstacles in achieving his potentiality. First, he saw that men seemed to be unequal in their capacity to rise to their full potential as children of God. "Man," he wrote in *The People's Case,* "is made in God's image or in a likeness, in judgment and will, unto God himself, according to the measure that in his nature he is proportioned and made capable to be the receiver and bearer thereof."[40] Also, he saw man constantly involved in a struggle with sin. Unlike some of the left-wing idealists of the time, he never denied that man had sinned and that even the best (including himself) would continue to do so. In their struggle God would help, for He had through Christ given man "an enlightened moral principle of judgment and will, opposite to and warring with the corrupt and degenerate past."[41] But in Vane's concept of man and also of government, he put great emphasis upon the part which man himself must play to develop and perfect himself and his government. He tells of his own personal striving in a letter to his wife written from prison on the Isle of Scilly. Man must develop his inward spirit, to become "all glorious within," and even those who have become so "must have their time of manifestation,

18

and be made all glorious without also." When this happens (which he admits has not yet been achieved by him) "then the whole body shall be full of light, having no part dark, as when the bright shining of a candle doth give thee light."[42]

The understanding of Vane's concept of man is essential for understanding his mature political theory. Maintaining that man was capable, with God's help, of rising to his full potential as a son of God, he nevertheless recognized that the struggle was constant and man's sin everpresent. The particular sin which Vane discussed again and again was self-interest, which, he tells us, "is no other than the spirit of man, lusting after the doing of his own will and procuring his own glory more than God's."[43] Believing as he did in the strength of man's self-interest, and the danger of any man possessing power, Vane never blamed God for man's shortcomings. Man, himself, he frequently asserted, is alone responsible for his own failure to rise to his potential as an individual or as a member of a group. "Our sins have been the cause, that our counsels, our forces, our wit, our conquests, and ourselves have been destructive to ourselves, to each other, and to a happy advancement towards our long and desired settlement."[44]

Vane's concept of a sinning man who yet possessed within himself and through God's grace the will and power to rise closer to his stature as a true child of God helps to explain his life-long concern with the spiritual freedom of man. The growth of the spirit could develop only when man was completely unhampered by the claims or demands of any individual group or government. Only an atmosphere of freedom and not of coercion could provide the setting in which man's spirit could become more like his Maker's.[45] This belief was one of the cornerstones of Vane's political thought.

Although he believed so profoundly in freedom, Vane was not an anarchist. He had served government for some time, but by 1653 had become disillusioned, and in *The Retired Man's Meditations* he devoted a whole chapter to government. Must government, he asked himself, run counter to God's plan; must it always impose the will of someone else on man? How could government be constructed and function so that it could be made a positive instrument for God's and man's purposes? What was the right relation between the individual and his government? Was obedience forced on man or freely willed by him for his own good? These questions were raised again in *A Healing Question* and in most of his later writings.

He convinced himself in *The Retired Man's Meditations* that government could be a positive good, actually instrumental in God's plan for man.

Government could also aid man to develop spiritually. "Government," he wrote "as in its primitive
constitution and right exercise, it hath its place and
bears its part in the reign and government of Christ
over men in this world."[46] Proper principles of governing stemmed from God, but man must first find
them and then work to establish and maintain them
on earth. By such work he was cooperating with
God and thereby playing his part in God's plan for
man. Of course an omnipotent God could construct
and impose right government on men, but might not
even God be a tyrant should He alone create right
government and then decree that men obey? Good
government had always from the beginning been
part of God's plan for man, but it was man's responsibility to discover it and set it up upon right principles.[47]

Right principles! In his earlier active career, he
had hinted at their importance. Now, in his more
formal writings, they became his main concern—
more vital than the particular form of the government or the details of its administration. I am "join-
ing in witness with you," he wrote Harrington,
"unto those principles of common right and freedom, that must be provided for, in whatsoever frame
of government it be, which does pretend to a perfection in its kind."[48] To discover and set forth those
principles became his major purpose,[49] as it had been

Plato's, and was to be Rousseau's. Because of his concern with right principles of governing, Vane merits greater recognition as a political philosopher than hitherto has been accorded him.

A first right principle of governing was recognition that man's spiritual freedom was absolute. Over this area only God rightly possessed authority. Without such freedom man could not develop to his full stature. Consequently, in right government, "the exercise thereof refers to the outward man, or outward concerns of man, in their bodily converse in this world."[50] Right government "is not to intrude itself into the office and proper concerns of Christ's inward government and rule in the conscience."[51]

> Unto this [spiritual] freedom the nations of this world have right and title, by the purchase of Christ's blood, who, by virtue of His death and resurrection, is become the sole Lord and Ruler in and over the conscience . . . For why shouldst thou set at naught thy brother in matters of his faith and conscience, and herein intrude into the proper office of Christ, since we are all to stand at the judgment-seat of Christ, whether governors or governed, and by His decision only are capable of being declared with certainty, to be in the right or in the wrong?"[52]

The line between the spiritual and civil must be an absolute one. No government of man over man could be right unless it recognized and accepted the fact that its authority could not touch man's spiritual freedom. For the magistrate to cross over that line was to act unjustly—to exceed his commission both from God and man. For the individual to be touched or constrained in his religious life was a denial of his spiritual nature and an impossible barrier in his striving for perfection. Equally important, society itself was harmed, for when religious freedom is denied, men "are nourished up in a biting, devouring, wrathful spirit, one against another, and are found transgressors of that royal law which forbids us to do that unto another which we would not have them do unto us, were we in their condition."[53] For society to be healthy, there must be complete respect for the individual's spiritual freedom. Protests against government in the name of spiritual freedom were common in this revolutionary period. No one, however, pointed out more clearly than Vane the complex nature of the problem: the wrong done to the individual whose spiritual freedom was denied and the harm done to society. Only when spiritual freedom was respected as an area over which jurisdiction belonged to God alone could there be a right government for the individual, and also for the group.

A second principle Vane insisted upon in right government was man's consent. Here again he was one of many who in this period regarded this concept as fundamental. Men as far apart in their ultimate views as Parker, Lilburne, and Hobbes, for example, made it central in their thinking. Vane's statements on this question are not always clear. He seemed to shift his ground; at times speaking of the people in general, at others of the good people, adherents like himself to the good cause.[54] Like Parker, he often identified the people with those represented in a Parliament possessing supremacy. Inexact as Vane's use of the term "people" is, his discussion of the concept, the consent of the people, reveals a grasp of its implications which to my knowledge were not seen clearly by any other thinker in this period, nor indeed before Rousseau.

No government can be based on right principles, Vane insisted, unless it rests on God's plan in which man's consent is essential. Man's first duty, he argued in *The Retired Man's Meditations,* is to grasp the truth that magistracy, as conceived by God, is good.

It will then be their desire and delight to inquire and consider in a way of free debate and common consent . . . how that which is the ordinance and institution of God, may become also the ordinance and statute of man, established in a free and natural way of common consent to the reuniting of all good men as one man in a happy union of their spirits, prayers and counsels to resist all common danger and opposition, which by devils or men may be raised against them.[55]

In *A Healing Question* he insisted that the time had come for good men to act and to establish in the England of their own day their consent to their own government. They should "set up meet persons in the place of supreme judicature and authority amongst them; whereby they may have the use and benefit of the choicest light and wisdom of the nation, that they are capable to call forth for rule and government under which they live . . ."[56] Again, in *A Needful Corrective* he made it clear that the best form of government rests upon "the common vote of the whole body." This consent, he continued,

> is the right door to enter into the exercise of supreme power, and is genuine, natural, righteous, consonant to those pure principles of man's nature, wherein he was first created, and does declare the governed to be in the state of free citizens, who as brethren partaking of the spirit of right reason, common to them as men made in the image of God, are equally entitled to their own oversight and government, and do therefore see cause voluntarily to associate themselves together, and on the grounds of common right and freedom, to agree to be subject and yield obedience to the laws, that from time to time made amongst them by their own free and common consent.[57]

Vane's idea of consent set forth in the above statement includes much: the relation between man as a child of God and the necessity of his consent to government; the nature of the associated group, and the problem of obedience. At this point the first two will be considered, and later the problem of obedience. Vane insisted that man's consent is the only "right door to enter into the exercise of supreme power." Men who are children of God are "entitled to their own exercise of supreme power." With this great privilege went great responsibilities. Man must not be passive but must act and create right government if he would realize his full potentiality. Furthermore, he must act as a child of God and as a rational being who sees "cause voluntarily to associate himself"[58] with others.

In *The Retired Man's Meditations* Vane set forth more fully his philosophy on the need and nature of this voluntary association among men. Here he wrote:

> . . . the subjection which God requires [is not] irrational and merely implicit, but rational and voluntary, unto which men are to be led not only by the awe and fear of God, unto whom it is they pay a duty; but are also to be won and persuaded by the sense of their common good and benefit thereby; which, in whatever forms the government be administered (that in themselves simply considered are all lawful and innocent) doth difference just and righteous rule and government over men, from a tyranny and subjection, unto private will and lust, which is none of God's ordinance, but the abuse of it.[59]

Vane's God recognizes the dignity of all men. His God does not arbitrarily create and designate some as rulers and others as subjects. Any subjection of man to government must be man's "rational" choice, his own voluntary acceptance of its common good and benefit. Passive acceptance is not enough, man himself must actively will it. As Vane wrote in his letter to Harrington, right government is seated "in the will of man" from which source, next to God Himself, it arises.[60]

When men will right government they associate themselves together as a group which is far more than a mere collection of separate individuals. Each man is first linked to God and through God to his brethren. Thus they become "knit together as one man"—to quote a biblical phrase Vane liked to use.[61] The group is now bound together, not by their fear of being destroyed without the protection of a great Leviathan, but by their tie with God Himself, in whose image each was cast. Through this link with God and with each other, the group is a harmonious one, bound together by their concern for the public welfare, by their respect for the spiritual freedom of each individual man, and by their dedication to a common cause. The group is made up of men "qualified thereunto, to act in righteousness and in fear of the Lord and in discharge of this his high and great trust."[62] It is a "reuniting of all good men as one man in a happy union of their spirits, prayers and counsels, to resist all common danger and opposition, which by devils or men may be raised against them."[63]

> Where there is then a righteous and good constitution of government, there is first an orderly union of many understandings together, as in the public and common supreme judicature or visible sovereignty set in a way of free and orderly exercise, for the directing and applying the use of the ruling power or the sword, to promote the interest and common welfare of the whole, without any disturbance or annoyance from within or without.[64]

For men to consent to government meant that men create an organic group of like hearts and spirits. A rational man, willing right government because he understands the need and its harmony with God's plan, must, if true to himself and his Creator, agree to put aside private interests and to act for the public welfare in concert with others who do likewise. By the act of association, he implicitly renounces his private interests. A man who uses his authority as part of a governing group to push his own private interests against others who also are children of God and with whom he is associated, would abandon his true Christian self. The result would be subjection, not freedom for himself, and tyranny, not right government for the group. Only by setting aside his private interests could man achieve true freedom both as an individual and as a member of a group. Only in this way could a governing group be rightly constituted, rightly exercise power, and rightly require obedience. Such an associated group possesses, because of its nature and the consent of each to it, respect for the individual. Above all, it must be supreme over the executive and military. Because of this supremacy, there is no need of specific fundamental laws aimed to protect the individual against the executive.

Vane's emphasis upon the supremacy of the group is a point which his commentators have seemed not to understand. At times, particularly in his trial and in some sections of *A Needful Corrective* and *The People's Case,* Vane spoke of limited government, of man's right to resist, and of fundamental laws to protect men's rights against the executive and his tyrannical military might. In *A Needful Corrective,* for example, he discussed an imperfect form of government "neither very good nor stark nought,"[65] where men "not able to be free men [as under right government] are resolved to do their utmost not to be slaves." Consequently they agree to be subject to the ruler "upon condition of enjoying certain known rights and privileges belonging to them as men, and which may distinguish them from mere slaves, and be laid as fundamental laws of that constitution of government."[66] Such a form, he explained, was the form of that monarchy of king, lords, and commons in 1640 which was an imperfect form.[67]

When, however, Vane was discussing or advocating a government based on right principles, as in *The Retired Man's Meditations,* in some sections of *A Healing Question* and of *A Needful Corrective,* and also in his Parliamentary speeches in 1659, he talked of the supremacy of the associated group "over the outward man." In *The Retired Man's Meditations* he stated that government is

> not to be in bondage to the judicials of Moses. . . . since the spirit and original pattern of those very judicials is set up by Christ in men through his resurrection from the dead; to enable them unto a righteous ruling over men. . . . And doubtless if Moses' judicials are thus to be left behind . . . no human ordinances or positive laws must expect to be perpetual and exempt from change and removal, if the Lord please by a visible hand of his own, in judgment and righteousness to fold them up as old garments . . .[68]

In *A Healing Question,* where his approach is less mystical, he also discussed supreme power:

> . . . the sovereignty [should] be acknowledged to reside originally in the whole body of adherents to the cause . . . and then . . . a supreme judicature [should] be set up and orderly constituted, as naturally arising and resulting from the free choice and consent of the whole body taken out from among

themselves, as flesh of their flesh, and bone of their bone, of the same public spirit and nature with themselves.[69]

Were this done, Vane argued, the actual administration would not be a problem, for the administrators, whether one or many, would not be supreme, but subordinate to the "supreme judicature," which would act for the people. In such a situation, he asked:

> Would a standing council of state settled for life in reference to the safety of the commonwealth, and for the maintaining intercourse and commerce with foreign states, under the inspection and oversight of the supreme judicature, but of the same fundamental constitution with themselves, would this be disliked [and viewed as arbitrary]?[70]

The answer was, of course, no. The form the executive should take (whether one or many) was unimportant, but its subordination to the supreme judicature was essential in government constructed on right principles of governing. In *A Needful Corrective* he again maintained that in right government the executive must be kept "within its due bounds" and that any organ of government exercising legislative power must be kept "within the power and consent of the people."[71]

When in 1659 Vane was a member of Richard Cromwell's Parliament, he argued that Parliament, which he identified with the people, rightly had the supremacy and was therefore in a position to define the Protector's position:

> . . . the office of right is in yourselves. It is in your hands, that you may have the honour of giving or not giving, as best likes you. . . . It therefore concerns you in this business, to have your eyes in your heads, to look well about you, that it not slip from you without considering what is your right, and the right of the people.[72]

This right had become theirs in full measure, Vane pointed out in 1659, with the end of kingship, when a free state had been established "to bring the people out of bondage," from all pretense of superiority over them. "It seemed plain to me" he explained, "that all offices had their rise from the people, and that all should be accountable to them. If this be monstrous, then it is monstrous to be safe and rational, and to bear your own good."[73] "If we can bear our own liberties," Vane contended, "we must accept this responsibility. We who are rightly supreme must rule ourselves. If we cannot accept this principle then "we will return to Egypt weary of our journey to Canaan."[74]

In a government resting on right principles, an associated people and their supreme judicature must also control the military. Vane was not an idealist who ignored the importance of the military, but he argued eloquently in *A Healing Question* against the possession and use of the military by a person or persons apart from and not subordinate to the people. Such a situation constituted tyranny, not freedom.

> This is that which make all sound and safe at the root, and gives the right balance necessary to be held up between sovereignty and subjection, in the exercise of all righteous government; applying the use of the sword to the promoting and upholding the public safety and welfare of the whole body, in preference, and, if need be, in opposition unto any of the parts . . .[75]

It was necessary, he insisted, that the people grasp the fact that the military is not dangerous when it is in right hands, in the hands of the people.

> For when once the whole body of the good people find that the military interest and capacity is their own, . . . they will presently see a necessity of continuing ever one with their army, raised and maintained by them for promoting this cause against the common enemy.[76]

Vane recognized also that when the holders of the sword were not subordinate to the associated group there was no stability in government. The minority group temporarily possessing the sword would lose out to another group "that on the next opportunity can lay hold on the sword. . . ." In this situation "the whole body" would be forced for a time "to serve and obey . . . the arbitrary will and judgment of those that bring themselves into rule by the power of the sword."[77] Force, according to Vane, is sometimes necessary, even useful, but in right government force must always be the might of an associated people, not of one leader or a minority group. It must be the servant and not the master of man. Above all, it must be a tool, always subordinate to, and never dominant over, the associated group. Individual man must obey armed might because he recognizes it as his own instrument, an active expression of the people's own rational decision.

Vane never explicitly and clearly discussed the question, but it would appear that he assumed that a government truly based on the right principles he had discovered and enunciated would not impose upon the spiritual freedom of any person. No associated group composed of men spiritually free could be a rightly associated group if the spiritual freedom of each was denied, for government exists only for the outward man.

Implicit in all of his political concepts discussed thus far is the question of obedience. This above all was the problem he had wrestled with in his active career and in his quiet meditations. The problem was essentially an ethical one. If man is God's child, his first and prime duty is to obey God.

For a rational man to give up his reason and will unto the judgment and will of another [man or men] (without which, no outward coercive power can be) whose judgment and will is not perfectly and unchangeably good and right is unwise and unsafe, and by the law of nature, forbidden.[78]

These words of Vane were written when he was considering government which did not yet rest on right principles of governing. ". . . there is no obligation to acknowledge obedience to a title you do not set up," he insisted in a Parliamentary speech in February, 1659.[79] When government does not rest on right principles, Vane certainly made it clear that one must obey God rather than man.

The situation is completely different, however, when government does rest on right principles. When a properly associated group respecting spiritual freedom controls both the executive and military, it rightly claims the obedience of all.

Where there is then a righteous and good constitution of government there is . . . a like union and readiness of will in all the individuals in their private capacities, to execute and obey (by all the power requisite and that they are able to put forth) those sovereign laws and orders issued out by their own deputies and trustees.[80]

When men consent to government and "associate themselves together" they "agree to be subject and yield obedience to the laws, that from time to time made amongst them by their own free and common consent."[81] If government is right, "the will that flows from such a judgment, is in its nature legislative and binding and of right to be obeyed for its own sake."[82] In these three statements, each taken from different tracts, Vane made it clear that men rightly owe obedience to right government. Since he viewed just government as a pattern of God's law, it is right for man to obey. In not obeying such a government men are "inexcusable . . . before God because the matter commanded is the matter of God's law and therefore just to be obeyed."[83] Obedience to such a government is obedience to God Himself. Obedience is also owed to right government because rational man recognizes that his government rests on right principles and that in obeying it he is acting as his rational self. In short, he is actually obeying his own best self.

The problem of obedience is a fundamental one in political society and in political thought. For centuries writers had raised the question of active and passive obedience to a higher authority, to king, emperor, or pope, but the problem of man obeying the authority willed and created by himself was a new one. Hobbes recognized the problem and gave one answer in the *Leviathan*. Vane saw the problem also but gave a very different answer. In fact, Vane was the only thinker, as far as I can discover, among the many advocates of more democratic government in the age of Cromwell who clearly saw and honestly faced the problem of man obeying himself. Some writers in this period seemed to assume naïvely that once the king's power was ended or sharply curtailed, new democratic governments would enact such good laws that obedience would naturally follow. The Levellers, however, must have been somewhat fearful of the laws even a democratic government might pass, for in the various Agreements of the People the Levellers listed an increasing number of specific areas which the peoples' representatives were expressly forbidden to touch. No Leveller writer, however, as far as I know, discussed as Vane did the problem of man obeying his own laws. It is a measure of Vane's stature as a political thinker that he recognized the problem and gave an answer consistent with his own basic beliefs. He insisted that in right government obedience is not a command by a higher authority, God or king, and is not sanctioned by external forces. It is, on the contrary, a recognition and willing acceptance by rational man himself of the necessity for him in his private capacity to accept the authority and laws passed by the associated group he has brought into being and of which he in his public capacity is a member. No government, according to Vane, possesses right principles unless right obedience is incorporated into its structure.

With such obedience an integral part of man's government, the age-old problem of governors and the governed disappears. For one or more to rule and others to be ruled is unethical, in accord neither with God's will nor with the dignity of man who had been made a spiritual brother of all his fellows. Although Vane abandoned the traditional view of a divinely sanctioned distinction between rulers and the ruled, he recognized that obedience is essential in organized society and set forth his own concept of that obedience which is consistent with man's nature and God's will. In his treatment of this problem of right obedience to the associated group which man himself under God had freely worked with others to create, Vane made his most profound and original contribution to political philosophy. His recognition of the problem came more than a century before Rousseau published the *Social Contract,* and his answer, though cast in the framework of Christian theology, is remarkably similar in some respects to Rousseau's treatment of man's freedom, the general will, and right obedience.[84]

Standing by His Principles

Once Vane had asked and given his answers to such searching questions he never abandoned them. Idealist though he was in so many aspects of his thought, he was realistically aware of the difficulties involved in actually setting up government based on right principles in the England of his own time. "We found great difficulties in the work," he said in 1659, "as most men are willing rather to sit down by slavery, than to buy themselves out of it at so great a price."[85] In the first place, he clearly saw that to achieve such a like-minded, public-spirited group, willing to direct its own destiny and obey its own dictates, was no easy task.[86] The primary difficulty as he conceived it was man's sin of self interest ". . . lusting after the doing of his own will and procuring his own glory more than God's." This had brought about man's fall, "setting up in him that great idol of self interest, which hath ever since so skillfully insinuated into the desire and heart of every natural man, that by its influence, the whole world seems to be governed, as well in religion as civil policy."[87]

In his letter to Harrington, Vane pointed out that citizens whose "equality in power is apt to make their tempers luxuriant and immoderate" have difficulty in reaching right agreements.[88] The greatest problem, he continues, "is to show how the depraved, corrupted and self-interested will of man, in the great body, which we call the people, being once left to its own free motion, shall be prevailed with to espouse their true public interest, and closely adhere to it, under the many trials and discouragements they must be sure to meet with before they obtain what they pursue."[89] Because of this great difficulty most men prefer to choose the "power of the sword moderately used, than to commit themselves to the boundless power of the people's will unbridled, and unsubjected unto any rules from inward principles or outward order and command."[90]

Men are all too likely, he pointed out in *A Needful Corrective,* to settle for halfway measures and accept rulers not of their own choosing who would promise to guarantee and respect certain rights of their subjects. This arrangement, however, meant that "such as are under it do seldom care to be better, they are so afraid that by attempting to mend themselves, they shall make themselves irrecoverably worse."[91] Vane viewed such a government as an imperfect one, not one which, according to God's plan, could be a positive good for man.

In spite of his penetrating understanding of the difficulty of setting up a government based on the principles of political right, Vane was convinced that it could and must be done. Although man had failed to establish such a government from 1649 to 1653, a second opportunity opened up in 1656 when Cromwell appeared to ask for help. Vane, believing that Cromwell sincerely wanted advice, wrote *A Healing Question* and sent it to him. In a revealing biographical paragraph at the end of *A Healing Question,* he makes clear the close connection be-

tween his ideas in *The Retired Man's Meditations*
and in *A Healing Question.*

> And because an essay [*The Retired Man's Medi-
> tations*] hath been already made in a private way to
> obtain the first thing, that is to say, conviction which
> chiefly is in the hand of the Lord to give; the same
> obligation lies upon the author, with respect to the
> second, for the exposing of it as now it is unto public
> view, and therein leaving it also with the Lord, for
> his blessing thereunto.[92]

Having worked out in general his basic ideas in *The
Retired Man's Meditations,* he turned in *A Healing
Question* to the more specific task of establishing
the government at this opportune moment upon
right principles of ruling.

In *A Healing Question* he clearly recognized that
the break between the military and the civil had
grown wider after the dissolution of the Commons
in 1653. Nevertheless, he was confident that the
breach could be healed and that all "good" men who
had once been united could come together again
and establish the government on those right principles upon which he had meditated and written in
The Retired Man's Meditations. The task can be
done, he argued fervently, since "the cause hath still
the same goodness in it as ever," which is to give the
people freedom to rule themselves and complete free-

dom in matters of religion, two principles basic in his political philosophy.[93] The good cause is God's cause and also the peoples', than which there can be no higher.

> Secondly [the task can be done because] the persons concerned and engaged in this cause are still the same as before, with the advantage of being more tried, more enured to danger and hardship, and more endeared to one another, by their various and great experiences, as well of their own hearts, as their fellow brethrens.[94] . . . They have showed themselves upon all occasions desirers and lovers of true freedom, either in civils or spirituals, or in both . . . which actions of their proceeding from the hearts sincerely affected to the cause, created in them a right to be of an incorporation and society by themselves, under the name of Good Party.[95]

Although a rift between some "good persons" and the army had developed, Vane argued that Cromwell and the army had only been tempted away from truth. With God's help, they, too, could see the light again and rejoin their brethren in healing the breach and setting up right government in the England of their day. The task could be done, Vane insisted, because God who had helped them in the past would not fail them now in advancing His own cause and theirs in building His government on earth.

To accomplish this great work of reconciliation Vane set forth in *A Healing Question* two proposals more specific than usually found in his writings. In one he dealt with the means by which spiritual freedom could be assured, and in the other he advocated that a constitutional convention be called to establish the government upon right principles. In the first of these proposals he followed up his eloquent plea for spiritual freedom, and for the necessity of the magistrate forbearing to meddle, with this suggestion:

> So that all care requisite for the peoples obtaining this [i.e. spiritual freedom] may be exercised with great ease, . . . and that this restraint be laid upon the supreme power before it be erected, as a fundamental constitution among others, upon which the free consent of the people is given to have the persons brought into the exercise of supreme authority over them, and on their behalf; and if besides, as a further confirmation hereunto, it be acknowledged the voluntary act of the ruling power, when once brought into a capacity of acting legislatively, that herein they are bound up and judge it their duty so to be (both in reference to God the institutor of magistracy, and in reference to the whole body by whom they are entrusted) this great blessing will hereby be so well provided for, that we shall have no cause to fear, as it may be ordered.[96]

Vane believed that spiritual freedom should be doubly guarded both by a "restraint upon the supreme power before it be erected" and also by the "ruling power" itself declaring "as a voluntary act" that it would not interfere with it. Man himself must take the responsibility and will right government which by its very nature has no right authority over the inner man.

Vane also proposed, in order to heal the breach between the civil and military party and "reunite" them, that a constitutional or constituent assembly should be called.

The most natural way for which would seem to be by a general council, or convention of faithful, honest, and discerning men, chosen for that purpose by the free consent of the whole body of adherents to this cause in the several parts of the nations, and observing the time and place of meeting appointed to them (with other circumstances concerning their election) by order from the present ruling power, but considered as general of the army.

Which convention is not properly to exercise the legislative power, but only to debate freely, and agree upon particulars; that, by way of fundamental constitutions, shall be laid and inviolably observed as the conditions upon which the whole body so represented doth consent to cast itself into a civil and politic incorporation, and under the visible form and administration of government therein declared, and to be by each individual member of the body subscribed in testimony of his of their particular con-

sent given thereunto. Which conditions so agreed
(and amongst them an act of oblivion for one) will
be without danger of being broken or departed from;
considering of what it is they are the conditions and
the nature of the convention wherein they are made,
which is of the people represented in their highest
state of sovereignty, as they have the sword in their
hands unsubjected unto the rules of civil government, but what themselves orderly assembled for that
purpose do think fit to make. And the sword upon
these conditions subjecting itself to the supreme judicature, thus to be set up: how suddenly might harmony, righteousness, love, peace, and safety unto the
whole body follow hereunto, as the happy fruit of
such a settlement, if the Lord have any delight to be
amongst us.[97]

In these paragraphs Vane set forth his proposal
for a constitutional convention, the first such proposal, as far as I know, ever to be made.[98] He left to
the party in power, Cromwell and the army, which
he disliked and distrusted, the initiative in calling
the convention. This concession is a clear indication
of his earnest desire to heal the breach and perhaps
also of his realism, flashing to the surface at times in
an amazing way. The convention itself, however, was
to be chosen freely by "the whole body of adherents
to the cause," obviously an elite group, but the best
qualified to establish the government upon right
principles. Possessing sovereignty over the outward

man with the military power or "sword in their hands," the elite group was to debate and set up the conditions upon which a rightly constituted government must rest. Vane clearly distinguished between the constitutional convention and the legislative power in the government to be created. He also insisted that the constitutional convention must set up not only the government but the conditions upon which it must operate. Such conditions must include the supremacy of the whole associated group or their representatives, "flesh of their flesh and bone of their bone," over the executive and military in any form of government to be set up. In fact the military must specifically and voluntarily, he seems to suggest, "subject itself to the supreme judicature" (or legislative body).

Although Vane does not explicitly mention spiritual freedom in his remarks concerning a constitutional convention, he had already made it clear in the earlier part of *A Healing Question* and also in *The Retired Man's Meditations* that no rightly constituted civil group has authority over the inner man. Spiritual freedom is an essential "condition" of any rightly constituted government. And finally, each member of the constituent body must give his individual consent to the arrangements made. By such consent, he both sets up his government and simultaneously agrees to obey what he himself has consti-

tuted. Rational obedience of all is thereby incorporated into the fundamental constitution.

Vane had become so convinced of the right principles for governing that he seemed to be confident
that a constitutional convention, made up of members of the chosen group or good party would insist
upon those principles and incorporate them in any
form of government to be set up. It is true, of course,
that Vane ignored many difficulties and problems
which would arise were an actual convention held.
He did not, for example, clearly indentify the "adherents to the cause" who were to choose the members, presumably from among themselves, for the
convention. One is perplexed by all his stress upon
a select group when all men are the children of God.
In *A Healing Question,* he explicitly limited the
men who chose the members of the constitutional
assembly to a select group who, if consistent with
their original principles, would choose men like
themselves, tried and true, as members of the convention and also of the supreme judicature. In his
other writings Vane sometimes spoke of the people
as a whole and at other times of a select group, making it virtually impossible to grasp the meaning of his
shift from one to the other.

His views, however, can perhaps be better understood if his varied approaches to problems are kept
in mind. As a religious mystic he believed pro-

foundly in the spiritual freedom of each man. As a political theorist he was concerned with right principles of governing. As a realist, however, he clearly recognized the great difficulties of setting up in his own time a government based on right principles. He actually spoke in *A Needful Corrective* of the dangers of the "peoples will unbridled."[99] At this particular time, therefore, when he hoped to heal the breach, only an elite group could make the right beginning. Members of such a group must be dedicated men, close to God, tried and true in their devotion to the cause. Only dedicated men were capable, Vane would maintain, of taking the full responsibility upon themselves of achieving an associated group, of putting public interests above private, of agreeing to obey themselves. In *A Needful Corrective* Vane throws some light on his own belief in an elite. It is essential, he explains,

> that in the time of the commonwealth's constituting, and in a nation much divided in affection and interest about their own government, none be admitted to the exercise of the right and privilege of a free citizen, for a season, but either such as are free born in respect of their holy and righteous principles, flowing from the birth of the spirit of God in them, restoring man in measure and degree, as at the first by creation unto the right of rule and dominion or else who, by their tried good affection and faithfulness to common right and public freedom, have de-

served to be trusted with the keeping or bearing their own arms in the public defense.[100]

Vane's belief that good government could be initiated only by a few, or by an elite, as he termed the group, was another form of the age-old concept of a wise legislator, to whom Plato, Machiavelli, and even Harrington and later Rousseau turned to initiate good government. Vane, in contrast to their emphasis upon one wise legislator, looked to a select group of indeterminate size for the right beginnings. The members of his select group had to be abundantly filled with the Spirit of God, if they were to lay right foundations. It is Vane the idealist and religious mystic speaking here. Once, however, the government was established and functioning, Vane certainly implied that more men, whom God would fill with His spirit, would become citizens or members of the associated sovereign group. To him all men as sons of God were potentially capable of sharing in governing themselves.

Not only is it difficult to establish right government, Vane pointed out, but it is equally hard to sustain it. In contrast to Machiavelli and Harrington, who maintained that a properly constructed government would last almost forever, Vane insisted that even right government needed the abundant and continuing grace of God. He approved of Harrington's plan in *The Commonwealth of Oceana* to

achieve freedom for man, but implied that a beauti-
fully designed system, such as Harrington's, lacked
the sustaining power necessary in any government,
however perfectly constructed, for its proper functioning. Vane recognized that Harrington, like himself, wanted the public good, not private interest, to
prevail. Harrington constructed his balanced government on such firm economic foundations and with
such carefully devised and detailed schemes for ini-
tiating policy and selecting alternatives that he opti-
mistically believed that this government would provide security and also that public interests would
prevail over private. By the soundness of its foundation and by the perfection of its construction, the
government of Oceana would continue to function
for a long, long time, perhaps forever, as its maker
intended it should.

Vane, however, realized that firm foundations
and a cleverly constructed superstructure were not
enough—

> what is that which is wanting [he asked] to balance
> and complete the motion of man's will, in the exer-
> cise of his own freedom, that it is so little to be
> trusted and relied on, in the pursuit of that which
> is the common interest of mankind and the public
> good of human societies? And if in this we search to
> the bottom, we have it declared in that Scripture,
> which says, it is not in man to order his own steps.

Man, at his best, stands in need of the balancing and
ruling motion of God's spirit to keep him steadfast.[101]

At all times, man, whether magistrate or representative, needs God's help. No nation can be really free
if it is alienated from God "by wicked works, how
much soever it be set at liberty in other respects, to
use the power of its own will in providing for its own
government." At all times "we are to take care in the
use of the ordinary means, daily afforded by God's
providence, that are most conducing to guide and
regulate the will of the people, unto their making of
good choice of the senate and their own deputies."[102]

When Vane wrote *A Healing Question* and *A
Needful Corrective* he was not a member of the government. By 1659, however, Oliver was dead and
Vane had been elected a member of Richard Cromwell's Parliament. Taking full advantage of the new
situation, Vane played a leading part in the great
debates of that winter concerning Richard's position.
Optimistic that another opportunity had been offered the "free people" of England assembled in
Parliament to establish right government, he again
set forth his political ideas. He saw the issue clearly,
posed the alternatives, and argued brilliantly for a
free state resting on the "people in Parliament."
None of the mysticism, so difficult to follow and
comprehend in *The Retired Man's Meditations,* is
here; nor any of the long involved sentences with

hidden or obscure meanings of *A Healing Question* or *A Needful Corrective*. In these parliamentary debates, Vane stands out as a clear thinker and brilliant exponent of the political principles he had earlier formulated. These were now set forth specifically and concretely in relation to the particular situation. Only by letting Vane speak for himself can the reader see him in his full stature.[103]

> I look upon it [Vane declared] as a special testimony of God's Providence that I am here to speak this before you [i.e., the Commons].[104]

> Consider what it is we are upon, a protector in the office of chief magistrate. But the office of right is in yourselves. It is in your hands, that you may have the honor of giving or not giving, as best likes you.[105]

> Ever since the execution of the king you have possessed the right to establish the government.[106]

> After the king's execution (an unavoidable necessity) it was then necessary for that little remnant of the Parliament, now the representative of the nation, to have resort to the foundation of all just power, and to create and establish a free state; to bring the people out of bondage, from all pretence of superiority over them. It seemed plain to me that all offices had their rise from the people, and that all should be accountable to them. If this be monstrous, then it is monstrous to be safe and rational and to bear your own good.[107]

[In the years between 1649 and 1653] we miscarried; . . . though this free state was shipwrecked, yet you have got a liberty left to say it is now again in your possession; else I am mistaken. If it be so, I hope you will not part with it, but upon grounds of wisdom and fidelity.[108]

. . . at the dissolution of the Long Parliament [i.e., 1653] you lost your possession, not your right.[109]

. . . The representative body never dies, whoever die.[110]

We again [in February 1659] have the opportunity to set up a free state and let us face the situation squarely. Do we or do we not want to take the responsibility upon ourselves to rule ourselves? If not, let us say so . . . If, however, you do wish to take advantage of this great opportunity again offered you, the foundation must be properly laid now.[111]

The whole debate runs upon these two feet, that at the same time you declare your judgements for his Highness, you would also assert the rights of the people. I believe you apprehend how dangerous it is to confess a title in being, that is not from yourselves, of your own giving; but by way of debt; for there is no obligation to acknowledge obedience to a title you do not set up. I would have it considered that such a vote be prepared that both may go together, and that it may pass with more unanimity.[112]

Assert your militia to be in you.[113]

First things come first, he argued in a debate on another issue.

> Honestly and uprightly make it your first business to settle your own constitution . . . I would have this to be your first business. To lay foundations. Obstructions in the foundation are dangerous.[114]

Vane never wavered from his point that again the time had come and the opportunity been given to lay the foundations of right government. Whatever the consequences or difficulties of such action might be, which some members of Parliament set forth, all could be overcome, because God was on their side.

> God is almighty: Will you not trust Him with the consequences? He that has unsettled a monarchy of so many descents, in peaceable times, and brought you to the top of your liberties, though he drive you back for a while into the wilderness, he will bring you back. He is a wiser workman than to reject his own work.[115]

In these debates Vane proclaimed no new political ideas. He set forth clearly the same principles of right government which he had previously explained in *The Retired Man's Meditations, A Healing Question,* and *A Needful Corrective.* Again he emphasized that the "dedicated" group in Parliament must establish proper foundations. They must see to it that the

new executive, Richard, was their own creature, subordinate to them. Only by such arrangements could
right government, insuring right obedience, be established. Vane remained so convinced of the rightness
of these principles, which were in accord with God's
plan for government for man that he was confident
that if man did his part God would support and
maintain "his own work" at this particular time in
English history.

During his active life, when he participated in
the councils of government, Vane worked for right
principles of governing, striving to discover and understand them, to make them clear to others, and
to take advantage of every opportunity to bring them
closer to realization in the England of his own day.
In the intervals when he withdrew from public life,
he continued his struggle to understand the ageless
problems of political society.

Living in the late Reformation period, his political thinking was shaped in part by the particular
problems and concepts of that age. Far to the left in
the Reformation spectrum of those seeking spiritual
freedom for the individual, he pleaded eloquently
for the inherent right of each man, a child of God,
to seek and worship God in his own way, free of any
restraint or control. Yet he was not a mere individu-
alist who resisted all organized authority, nor did he

accept it without question. The community was as important to him as the individual. Like Calvin, Vane was concerned that the community be a holy one. Like Augustine, he looked for a City of God, but believed that his heavenly city could be established on earth.[116] He wrote to Harrington in *A Needful Corrective* that he wanted to perfect Harrington's principles of true freedom "to the rendering us a holy as well as a free people."[117] There was always, in Vane's thinking, a close tie between the individual and the community. Only right-minded individuals could create and sustain such a community, and they constantly needed God's grace. Once right government existed, however, it acted as a positive good, assisting God's and man's purposes.

Believing almost fanatically in spiritual freedom, he denied that civil government could rightly exercise authority over man's spirit. In civil affairs he insisted on a form of association which must by its very nature provide both authority for the group and freedom for each member, since each must consent to it. Keenly aware of man's besetting sin of self-interest, he still insisted that a publicly minded group could and must be created. Like Plato,[118] he insisted that true rulers must put the public interest first, but Vane's elite group of men needed God's grace rather than special education to keep them constantly striving for the public welfare. Afraid of sovereign power because he saw it could so easily tyrannize over men, he nevertheless refused to settle for anything less. Power, when rightly organized, resting on man's consent, must be sovereign over the outward man and not resisted. Force wielded by such a power was moral. Obedience to such a power was right because man who had willed and created it was obeying God himself and other like-minded men, also children of God, joined together with him in an organic association. In this age of conflicting loyalties no one, as far as I know, probed as deeply as Vane into the ethical problem of obedience. He was, in short, a political theorist of considerable stature whose name should be added to the other illustrious thinkers who made this age one of the great creative periods in the history of political thought.

Vane's Political Thought in Retrospect

In the last three years of his life, from the time of the failure of the republic in 1659 until his own execution in 1662, Vane remained true to the principles of political theory he had enunciated. At times, he seems to have despaired of achieving them in the England of his own day, but he never lost faith that they were in accord with God's plan for mankind, and that God could and would, in some way and at some time, bring them about. Vane continued to meditate and write about the cause he had long espoused. He examined and tested in retrospect the views he had earlier held and the part he himself had played in the great events beginning in 1640, insisting that all along he had acted consistently in accord with his fundamental principles. In his later writings, therefore, he does throw light on some aspects of his own career and helps the historian who has understood his political theory to see more clearly into some of the dim corners of his past career. In the final part of this essay, therefore, several ways in which our understanding of Vane and English history in this period can be illuminated by this study of his political ideas will be suggested.

Vane's interpretation of his own role and Parliament's role from 1640 to the execution of the king is found in *The People's Case,* in the material prepared for his own trial, to some extent in *A Healing Question,* and in several shorter writings.[119] Vane explained that the principles upon which the government of England had rested before the Civil War were not entirely wrong. On the contrary, the government had met the test in some respects of those political principles he had set forth as essential for right government. He recognized that the king had been the chief executive possessing a considerable amount of power, although Vane did not discuss its exact extent. He insisted, however, that the people also had for a long time possessed a good deal of power in Parliament.

> God doth allow and confer by the very law of nature, upon the *community* or body of the people (that are related to, and concerned in the right of government, placed over them) the liberty by their common vote or suffrage duly given, to be assenters or dissenters thereunto, and to affirm and make stable or disallow and render ineffectual, what shall apparently be found by them to be for the good or hurt of that *society* whose welfare are next under the justice of God's commands and His glory, in the supreme law, and the very end of all subordinate governing power.[120]

So important were the people or *society* that when the king made an agreement with Parliament, his government was just and the peoples' obedience right. "The agreements or laws reached between the king and the subject are," Vane explained, "the standards unto the king's rule and the peoples' obedience, signifying the justice of his commands, and the dueness of their allegiance."[121]

> The will that flows from such a judgment is in its nature legislative, and binding, and of right to be obeyed for its own sake, and the perfection it carries in it and with it, in all its actings.[122]

In this statement Vane has included two of his fundamental political principles. He has made it clear that when king, lords, and commons agree, their legislative act or will is supreme. Also, that here is one form of government which men should obey because its underlying principles are sound.

To insure the continued importance of Parliament in such a supreme government and to prevent the king from deserting the counsel of Parliament and following his private rather than his public judgment, Parliament had passed in 1641 the act against its dissolution without its own consent.[123] This act, Vane maintains, was one of the important steps forward in the restoring of "the nation to their original right, and just natural liberty."[124] He went on to explain that in the Grand Remonstrance, Parliament had set forth the justice of their cause.[125] He cleverly quoted the king's answer to the Nineteen Propositions in which the king said:

> The laws of this kingdom are made by a king, a house of peers, and a house of commons, chosen by the people, all having free vote, and particular privilege. These three estates making one incorporate body, are they, in whom the sovereignty and supreme power is placed, as to the making and repealing of laws.[126]

The sovereignty, in other words, Vane contended, had been a mixed one, and when no agreement among the sharers of sovereignty could be reached, war eventually resulted.

Vane, of course, had sided with Parliament in the war, but in his theoretical justifications of Parliament's position he was more moderate than many of Parliament's champions, than, for example, Henry Parker, Charles Herle, John Goodwin, or Samuel Rutherford. Like Philip Hunton,[127] Vane insisted that here was a dilemma for which English law did not provide a clear answer. If the three estates disagreed to the point where only war was the answer, "it is not possible for any man to proceed according to all formalities of law."[128] And again he said, "When new and never heard of changes do fall out in the kingdom, it is not likely that the known and written laws of the land should be the exact rule."[129] Although Vane maintained that the law did not clearly provide for the existing situation, he insisted that the Parliament's position or "cause" was a just and righteous one. In presenting the rightness of its cause, Vane used his concept of an associated people, and for all practical purposes, identified lords and commons with it. Parliament, he maintained, was pursuing "the true good and welfare of the whole body or community as their end."[130] Their purpose was right for they were providing the protection which government should give.

Like other writers supporting Parliament's cause, Vane called also upon the law of nature to justify Parliament's action. His interpretation, however, of the law of nature is unique in certain ways. Also, it is in conformity with his political philosophy. It is

> to wit, that law which God, at the creation of man, infused into his heart for his preservation and direction, the law eternal. Yet it is not this law, as it is in the heart of every individual man, that is binding over many; or legislative, but as it is the act of a *community, or an associated people,* by the right dictates and persuasion of the work of this law in their hearts. . . . This is that which chancellor Fortescue calls political power here in England, by which, as by the ordinance of man, in pursuance of the ordinance of God, the regal office is constituted; or the king's politic capacity, and becomes appropriated to his natural person.[131]

Parliament's cause in the Civil War was right because they had acted as an "associated people" in accord with principles God had implanted in their hearts. To act against the will of such a community was wrong—"the going against which is, in nature as well as by the law of nations, an offence of the highest rank among men. For it must be presumed, that there is more of the wisdom and will of God in that public suffrage of the whole nation than of any private person or lesser collective body."[132] To resist the judgment of such a body, he implies, is to resist the judgment of God. He himself had obeyed Parliament and in so doing, had kept "his station and place of trust, wherein God and the law did set him."[133] He had been concerned "that no detriment in the general come into the commonwealth by the failure of justice and the necessary protection due from government."[134] Because its cause was just and in accord with the principles of God, Vane implied, God had given Parliament the victory and by that victory their rational right to rule themselves had been strengthened.[135] In this justification of Parliament's stand from 1640 to 1649, Vane emphasized the idea of Parliament's rightness because it was a community. It is noteworthy that he turned to Fortescue's concept of political power to undergird such a justification. Vane, in other words, like so many radicals in this revolutionary period, looked backward as well as forward. He was both a Burke and a Rousseau. He had found that certain good principles of government had long been established in England from which the king had departed and for which Parliament had continued to stand. He had hoped a way might be found of continuing a government which included a king, but a king with no power which could be used arbitrarily against his people. Power which did not rise from the community and remain subordinate to it could all too easily become tyrannical.

By December 1648, Vane had come to the conclusion that no satisfactory agreement with Charles could be reached which would prevent him "or his successors" from exercising "as tyrannical a government" as he had formerly carried on.[136] Although Vane had urged at this time that Parliament should "proceed to the settling of government without him"[137] (i.e., Charles), the record of his own activities and thoughts during these critical weeks is meager. It is known that he retired, refusing to take part in a Parliament which sanctioned the trial and execution of the king. Ten years later, in 1659, he explained this action: "I confess I was then exceedingly to seek, in the clearness of my judgment, as to the trial of the king. I was for six weeks absent from my seat here, out of my tenderness of blood."[138] This statement on such a critical matter is tantalizingly brief, but Vane refused to explain more. While his reference to his "tenderness of blood" has been used by historians seeking to understand his withdrawal at this critical time, his statement that he was seeking to clarify his own understanding of the meaning of the trial of the king has not been given sufficient attention by historians.

Dark and unclear as the actual historical record seems to be, some light may be shed on his thoughts at this critical time by turning to the principles of government he later enunciated and toward which he was moving in 1649. It seems apparent that his later political theory helps to explain his earlier actions.

In his trial and in *The People's Case* he claimed that a government headed by a king could become a right one if the king wielded only subordinate power to his people in Parliament. Principles of government always meant more to Vane than forms or details. While on December 8 he had urged that the time had come for Parliament to move ahead without the king, he must have recognized that ties with the past would have to be broken and new foundations laid. Now, if ever, such foundations must be rightly established. But could they be, he may have asked, if the king were brought to trial and executed by a Parliament whose claim of resting on the people's consent was more doubtful than ever after Pride's Purge when the army (or sword) had forcibly intervened? At his trial in 1662 Vane explicitly spoke of the "force of arms," preventing some members from entering the house. This was the reason he himself "forbear to come to the Parliament for the space of ten weeks."[139] In his mature political philosophy, Vane always insisted that military might, although sometimes necessary in human affairs, must rightly be subordinate to an associated people. Was he not asking himself in those critical weeks in 1648–1649, when he absented himself from the Commons, whether a supreme people was acting freely or under the threat of military might? In the face of uncertainty concerning such a vital matter,

his withdrawal to meditate upon the principles involved in the rapid sequence of events is understandable. He must have believed that he should play no
part in such doubtful actions at a time when old
foundations were being destroyed and new ones laid.
Any government, even one of the people, might be
tainted, or at least not rightly established, if force
played a part in its origin. Questions and doubts
such as I have suggested may well have gone through
Vane's mind, for they are consistent with the political principles he later worked out and set forth.

In 1659 Vane, speaking in Parliament, put into
words his clear awareness of the serious implications
of the king's execution. It meant to him that the
people in Parliament, recognizing their full responsibility for their own welfare, had acted. Having
taken upon themselves that awesome responsibility,
they must live up to it.

> If you be not now satisfied with this business [i.e. the
> king's execution, he stated in February 1659], you
> will put a strange construction upon that action, and
> upon all that has been done by the general and sol-
> diers. If you, here, will now doubt this right to be in
> you, you draw the guilt upon the body of the whole
> nation . . . It will be questioned whether that was
> an act of justice or murder.[140]

There is one short tract, *Ancient Foundations,* in
which Vane throws additional light on his struggle

with himself. Believing as Vane did that the traditional English government contained the essential
foundations for right government, which the king
should be brought to see, he was understandably
reluctant to abandon the existing form of king,
lords, and commons. And yet, perhaps God had so
willed.

> Ancient foundations [he wrote] whence once [they]
> become destructive to those very ends for which they
> were first ordained, and prove hindrances, to the good
> and enjoyment of humane societies, to the true wor-
> ship of God and the safety of the people, are for their
> sakes, and upon the same reasons to be altered, for
> which they were first laid. In the way of God's justice
> they may be shaken and removed, in order to accom-
> plish the counsels of his will, upon such a state, na-
> tion, or kingdom, in order to his introducing a right-
> eous government, of his own framing.[141]

By the time Vane wrote this tract, which it is
impossible to date, he seems to have convinced himself that ancient foundations must sometimes be
altered. In 1649, however, Vane had not thought out
the dilemma as clearly as he later saw and stated it.
He was, in 1649, still seeking the right answer and
could only, if true to himself, withdraw from the
whole situation.

Uncertain as Vane seemed to be whether or not

man had acted rightly in executing the king, he came to accept and serve the Commonwealth. How could he play this role, one may ask, since he was such an idealist? In answering this question, it must be remembered that Vane was both a realist and an idealist. Tainted as perhaps he believed its origins to be, he accepted the Commonwealth. In the first place the community needed protection. Here Vane was thinking as a practical politician. Furthermore, God had given man this great opportunity to rule himself and man should prove that he was worthy of God's providence. The Parliament which continued from 1649 to 1653, he explained in *Ancient Foundations,*

> might have performed things necessary at present, for the safety and preservation of the body they represented. They might have been a good help to settle righteous government, in a constitution most acceptable to God, and beneficial to the governed, on the foundation of God's institution, and the peoples' ordination, in consent together, laid by the power of God and the peoples' own swords, in the hands of their faithful trustees.[142]

Without God's support they would not have been able to have had this great opportunity. God had helped "in their times of greatest confusion." "In the flames of a Civil War" they had not been "consumed."[143] God had constantly watched over them,

waiting for man to act rightly. But man had failed
to do his part in those years between 1649 and 1653.

Vane believed profoundly that man should act.
Man should always pray for God to bring about
righteous government, but man himself, a child of
God, must do his duty and act in cooperation with
God. Faith should show itself by works. As he wrote
in *The Retired Man's Meditations:*

> . . . there is a duty of the day, a generation-work,
> respecting the time and circumstances of action, in
> which the lot of our life is cast, which calls upon us
> to use all lawful and righteous means that are af-
> forded by the good hand of God, through the inward
> light and knowledge he vouchsafes, and outward
> providence and helps which he casts in, whereby to
> make way for, and to be hasting unto the coming of
> that day of God wherein the old heavens and earth
> shall be rolled away as garments, yea, with the works
> that are therein, be burnt up, and the new heavens
> and the new earth wherein dwelleth righteousness
> shall be brought forth in their room . . . we are to be
> using all lawful means and endeavours, to come as
> near the primitive pattern and rule as we can, in our
> whole practice throughout.[144]

"A generation-work!" This phrase explains much.
It helps us to see that once he had worked out the
principles of right government, he maintained that
it was his first duty to use every opportunity to bring
them about. Any immediate decision must always be

made in the light of his responsibility to promote the cause of God and establish right government in the England of his day.[145] He explained that he had worked for the Commonwealth as long as he believed it to be moving in the right direction. He had known that men might err and would always be sorely tempted, but he had continued to hope that they would return to the right way. When sharp divisions among the members of Parliament had grown, when Cromwell in 1653 had used the sword to dissolve the Rump, Vane had become more attached, even fanatically so, to the remnant of the faithful supporters of Parliament to whom he had looked to establish the principles of right government. He regarded the faithful adherents to the cause as the elite, who must not be dispersed, but must be continued as members of Parliament in a new election. They must be there both to preserve the link with the past and also to guide the new Parliament and its members in the right way. It was still possible for a commonwealth based on right principles to be established. To this belief he clung desperately. It had become an obsession with him from which he would not part even though it meant a rift between himself and Cromwell.

No attempt will be made in this article, concerned primarily with Vane as a political theorist, to evaluate his character, so baffling to his contemporaries and also to later historians. It is relevant, however, to suggest that a future biographer must take account of Vane's political ideas in any interpretation of the man. Right principles of governing were fundamental to Vane, and so also was his belief in a "generation-work." On the one hand, Vane was a mystic and idealist, whose utopian views on government seem not to have been really understood by his contemporaries or later historians.[146] On the other hand, Vane, like the author of the *Utopia,* was a realist who believed in serving his own generation. Vane hoped that by such service he might help the government of his own time to move ahead, even if slowly, toward its desired end. His utopian views and practical actions do not seem essentially contradictory in the light of his own interpretation of the relation between the two.

There are other seeming contradictions which the future biographer must face in any evaluation of Vane's intellectual ability. Even Clarendon admits that "in all matters without the verge of religion . . . his reason and understanding . . . was inferior to that of few men,"[147] and that he "discerned the purposes of other men with wonderful sagacity."[148] Clarendon also wrote of Vane's "profound dissimulation."[149] In his last book Godfrey Davies referred to Vane as an "adroit politician and a mystic, clearheaded in politics if cloudy in religion."[150] Neither

the seventeenth- or twentieth-century historian seems
to have been aware of the close connection between
Vane's religious and political views. Their integral
relationship should not be ignored by a future
biographer.

From a study of Vane's ideas, it is understandable
why the words "dissimulate" and "adroit" have been
used to describe this man. Particularly in his trial
and in *The People's Case* he cleverly turned to
English law and legal traditions and writings in defense of his own behavior. Yet he adroitly and subtly
shifted whenever necessary in his argument from
legal maxims to political principles. To Clarendon
and the Royalists on the right his shift from one to
the other surely appeared tricky, although they must
also have recognized and been fearful of the bril-
liance of this man who might still, if left alive,
threaten the new regime of Charles II.

No wonder also that the Levellers on the left had
all along regarded Vane as one of their worst enemies. He, unlike John Lilburne, Richard Overton,
John Wildman, and other Leveller writers, saw
some good in the established government of king,
lords, and commons. Even when he reluctantly ad-
mitted that the king's actions made it impossible for
such a form of government to progress toward a
more perfect one, he did not, as the Levellers did,
talk of a state of nature from which an entirely fresh

start should be made. He still clung to the belief that the small remnant of those elected members of Parliament was essential for achieving right principles of governing. Leveller pamphleteers who hated the government of the commonwealth and all who participated in it must have had no realization that Vane's views of the right government he hoped man would establish were even more utopian than their own.[151]

Perhaps the most significant chapter in a future biography of Vane will be an account of the relations between Vane and Cromwell. A close study of Vane's political principles has given me some insight into that fascinating story of the growing animosity between the two men who had for years worked together and shared many similar aspirations and thoughts. Vane was a political philosopher, whereas Cromwell was not. Both believed in God's providence but did not always agree in the interpretation of it. To Cromwell, God's providence did not always speak clearly, particularly when it involved a difficult decision. In each of his major dilemmas—to kill the king, to dissolve the Rump, and to refuse the crown—Cromwell hesitated. Was it God or the devil speaking? And did providence clearly point only one way? Did it point to the Parliament or to the army as the human institution which Cromwell should employ in carrying out the opportunities offered by

God's providence? What part did events, particularly his own military successes, play in making God's providence clear?

To Vane, Cromwell himself played too active and too personal a part in the events whose success he later came to attribute to divine providence. Vane was not satisfied with Cromwell's "self-establishing principles."[152] Before 1655 Vane may have been tortured, as Cromwell was, by doubts concerning manifestations of God's providence, but he had waited "passively" to determine whether God had spoken clearly. After 1655, however, when in his retirement he had thought out and enunciated his political principles, the doubts no longer prevailed. As he reviewed the situation in the years beginning in January, 1649, both God's providence and man's responsibility became clear. God, he maintained, had assisted man in Parliament's victory, and now man himself must take the responsibility to establish government based upon right principles in accord with God's plan for mankind. This was the cause or mission of those who by their actions had proved their fitness to guide Englishmen toward right government. Vane paid Cromwell the compliment of implying that Cromwell still belonged to this group. Only the temptation to power had temporarily diverted him from pursuing the cause.

With these differences in mind, it may be suggested that Vane was more disturbed in some respects by Cromwell's actions and policies than by Charles's. When Charles had been king, Vane believed that England was only progressing toward the true commonwealth. With Parliament's victory and Charles's death, however, the way was clear for Englishmen true to the cause, as he believed Cromwell once had been and still could be, to rise to their full stature and cooperate with God to establish His right principles of governing. Instead, Cromwell and other officers of that army which had been raised by the peoples' representatives, the Parliament, and to whom God had given the victory, had used the sword against the party of which they had been members. They had betrayed their great trust, allowing private self-interest to prevail against the public good and military might to "tyrannize" over civil government. Such action was a greater sin in Vane's eyes than Charles's, because Cromwell had once been a trusted member and leader of the cause. Vane reminded Cromwell of his sins in an impassioned letter, the key parts of which are here presented.[153]

> . . . I desire to speak before your own conscience in the sight of God, . . . I am so little satisfied with your active, and self-establishing principles, in the lively colors wherein daily they show themselves, as you are

or can be with my passive ones, and am willing in
this to join issue with you, and to beg of the Lord to
judge between us and to give the decision according
to truth and right conscience.

. . . Governors themselves are neither to be, nor make
themselves more than what in truth and righteousness they are and ought to be: when they swerve from
this rule, they become sinners and must look by
transgression to fall, as well as the lowest of the
people.

That which in truth of fact you were, is visible
enough to every eye, that is to say, under the legislative authority of the people represented in Parliament, duly chosen and rightly constituted: you and
the force under your command are the nations
strength and formed military power, kept up at a
settled pay to be employed for the nation's use and
service by a derived authority from them. . . . This
then is the power which duly and properly you are
and more than this, I am not satisfied in my conscience is in truth and righteousness appertaining
unto you; to use this power lawfully, is your honor,
your duty, your safety . . . And although your own
conscience cannot but consent to the truth of what
is here told you, in the name and fear of the Lord,
yet being strong, and trusting to the power of your
sword, which is flesh and not spirit, is man and not
God, your heart is lifted up, if you speedily repent
not, unto your destruction; . . .

. . . to the good people of this nation in Parliament
assembled, and rightly constituted who were, and
ought to be your earthly head; you lift up your heel,

and harden your self every day more than other, in a fixed resolution not to become subject, as is your duty, nor to hold and keep yourself in your due station allotted to you in the body: but are aiming at the throne in spirituals as well as temporals: and to set your-self in a capacity of not holding your head either in the one consideration or the other . . .

Take then in good part before it be too late, this faithful warning and following advice of an ancient friend, but is now thought fit to be used and dealt with as an enemy.

Break off timely your sins by repentance, do judgment, execute justice, and walk humbly before the Lord.[154]

Because Cromwell's government of the Protectorate was not constituted on right principles, nor even working toward them, Vane could not believe that any good could come of it.

. . . if there be never so many fair branches of liberty planted on the root of a private and selfish interest, they will not long prosper, but must within a little time wither and degenerate into the nature of that whereunto they are planted.[155]

The goodness of any cause is not merely to be judged by the events, whether visibly prosperous or unprosperous, but by the righteousness of its principles.[156]

Cromwell's major sin, according to Vane, was his refusal to subordinate the military to the civil. However good the ends were for which Cromwell used

77

the military, whatever successes England under the Protectorate achieved, they could not be justified since the government was wrongly constructed. Individual and collective man could rightly obey armed might only if he recognized it as his own instrument, an active expression of the peoples' own rational decision. Man could not be coerced into goodness by a force which he himself had not established and whose use he had not sanctioned. Cromwell's "self-establishing principles" were anathema to Vane. Right principles must be established by man, but only in cooperation with other rational men associating together in accord with the principles of God.

Vane, committed to absolute spiritual freedom, could not approve of or accept Cromwell's religious policies, although they were the most definite steps toward toleration that had yet been taken in England. Cromwell still maintained a state church supported by tithes, even though several Protestant groups, not just one, enjoyed the livings. Anglicans, Catholics, and even Jews were in general treated with moderation. Yet Vane saw Cromwell's religious policies as only makeshift devices. They were a far cry from true religious freedom where an associated people solemnly pronounced that the realm of the spirit belonged only to God and not to man. For the governing group to grant spiritual freedom would imply that the group rightly possessed the authority to deny such freedom, and to Vane such authority did not rightly belong to man at all. Furthermore, for Cromwell to rely upon his own military power to dissolve a parliament which would not support the degree of religious toleration he himself and the council of state had established, was compounding the wrong. Not by force, but only by the rational will of men could true religious freedom be achieved.

If Vane's attitude toward Cromwell is illuminated by viewing it through the spectacles of Vane's right principles, so also can Cromwell's attitude toward Vane be better understood if Vane's principles are kept in mind. Cromwell must have been perplexed and infuriated by the self-righteousness of Vane, his refusal to compromise, his insistence that the military must never be used against a people whose behavior fell far short of Vane's idealization of them. Why could not Vane who, as a leader in the government, had shown an amazing grasp of political forces, realize the practical problems with which he, Cromwell, was grappling? Vane, now out of power, reminded Cromwell of his own earlier thoughts and aspirations. He, Cromwell, still had high ideals and worthy objectives, but he had become increasingly aware, year by year, of the difficulties of achieving them. Much as Cromwell desired

to establish constitutional, limited civilian rule, he
wished even more to set up as much religious toleration as the political situation and the climate of
opinion allowed. When the Protectorate Parliaments
did not cooperate but worked to overthrow his religious program, Cromwell reluctantly turned to the
army. Was not it also the handiwork of God? Could
he, Cromwell, refuse God's calling? How could Vane
be so certain that God revealed His will in only one
right way? Was not God omnipotent, choosing di-
verse ways to lead His people and His servant, Cromwell? Questions such as these can only be conjec-
tured, not documented, but they are questions which
seem consistent with Cromwell's own beliefs and
policies. And yet perhaps all along Cromwell still
held on to an unconscious sense of guilt that he had
not been true to the cause, whereas Vane had.

We do know, however, that as Cromwell grew
older the tasks of government became more difficult.
He who in the Putney Debates in 1647 had hoped
that through discussion God would illuminate men's
minds and show the way to unity, was still seeking,
even on his deathbed, as his last prayer reveals.[157] In
the interval, however, when he had wielded power,
he more and more came to realize how difficult it
was to move ahead and do good. "I am a man stand-
ing in the place I am in, which place I undertook
not so much out of hope of doing any good, as out of

a desire to prevent mischief and evil, which I see
was imminent in the nation.''[158]

Here was his fundamental difference with Vane.
As the years went on and Cromwell struggled with
his task of governing a sorely divided England, the
rift between him and Vane widened. Not only was
Vane fourteen years younger, but he was more and
more determined, since writing *The Retired Man's
Meditations,* that government could only be good if
established on right principles. As Vane became
more dogmatic, Cromwell became more pragmatic.
As Vane insisted that right government must be established on earth, Cromwell seemed resigned just
to hold his government together, faulty as its construction and policies might be. These men, who
once had been close friends, moved farther and farther apart. Cromwell must have despaired, as Vane
seldom did, of man ever establishing on earth a
government based on right principles.

NOTES

[1] The first biographer of Vane was his friend George Sykes, whose *Life and Death of Sir Henry Vane, or a Short Narrative of the Main Passages of his Earthly Pilgrimmage* appeared in 1662, the year of Vane's execution. In *The Statesmen of the Commonwealth of England* (New York, 1846), 265–353, John Forster shows real understanding of some aspects of Vane's career and thought. Among the other biographies the two best are, in my judgment, by F. J. C. Hearnshaw, 1910, and J. K. Hosmer, 1888. C. H. Firth's account of Vane in the *Dictionary of National Biography* is valuable, but gives little attention to Vane as a theorist. The most significant facts concerning his earlier years are the following. Vane, born in 1613, was a gentleman, the eldest son of Sir Henry Vane Senior, who served Charles I as diplomat, member of the privy council, and secretary of state. Vane the Younger attended school at Westminster and later spent a short time at Oxford, and probably at Geneva. When he was only fourteen or fifteen he became a convinced Puritan and remained one all his life. In 1635 his Puritan convictions influenced him to emigrate to Massachusetts; because of his high birth he was elected governor of the colony in 1636. He became involved in the Anne Hutchinson controversy and his sympathy with her views was one reason for his failure to be re-elected governor in 1637. In that year he returned to England and in 1640 was elected a member of the Commons in both the Short and Long Parliaments. He was a religious mystic, probably a seeker who cannot be identified as belonging to any one sect. Whether he was ever a Fifth Monarchist is uncertain.

[2] In this introductory material I have used only standard sources, both primary and secondary, not attempting to add to our knowledge or interpretation of him, but only to present briefly the most basic ideas he actually enunciated in speeches and letters in the years between 1637 and his retirement from public life in 1653. None of his formal writings came during this period.

[3] *Hutchinson Papers*, 2 vols. (Prince Society, 1864), I, 84–96.

[4] *Ibid.*, 95. I have modernized the spelling and capitalization of all direct quotations taken from Vane's writings and speeches.

[5] *Ibid.*, 88.

[6] *Ibid.*, 84.

[7] *Ibid.*, 96.

[8] *Sir Henry Vane, His Speech in the House of Commons, at a Committee for the Bill against Episcopal Government* . . . June 11, 1641, London, 1641, 5.

[9] *Ibid.*, 2.

[10] *Ibid.*, 9.

[11] In the latter part of his doctoral thesis, *The Rise of the Independent Party*, J. Hexter is doubtful that there is sufficient evidence to indicate that Vane was responsible for injecting these words (p. 196).

[12] R. Baillie, *Letters and Journals*, II, 235–37, quoted by W. A. Shaw, *A History of the English Church during the Civil Wars and under the Commonwealth 1640–1660*. 2 vols. (London, 1900), I, 41.

[13] S. R. Gardiner, *History of the Great Civil War, 1642–1649*, 4 vols. (London, 1904–1905), IV, 217.

[14] According to W. C. Abbott, *The Writings and Speeches of Oliver Cromwell*, 4 vols. (Cambridge, Mass., 1937–47), I, 41. In his own trial in 1662, Vane claimed that the purpose of the "cause" was set forth in the *Grand Remonstrance* (T. B. Howell, ed., *Cobbett's Complete Collection of State Trials*, 33 vols. [London, 1809–26], VI, 194, 196). Later cited as *State Trials*.

[15] C. H. Firth, Vane the Younger in *D. N. B.*

[16] *The Parliamentary or Constitutional History of England*, 1753, XVIII, 291.

[17] *Ibid.*

[18] See pages 65–67.

[19] S. R. Gardiner, *History of the Commonwealth and Protectorate, 1649–1656*, 4 vols. (London, 1903), I, 6, 7.

[20] It is difficult to understand why Gardiner's history of the period dealing with the years from 1649 to 1653 pays relatively little attention to Vane. Older historians, Godwin and Forster, seem to recognize his importance more than Gardiner (W. Godwin, *History of the Commonwealth of England*, 4 vols. [London, 1824–28]; Forster, *Statesmen*.

[21] Given in Gardiner, *History of the Commonwealth*, II, 104.

[22] Forster, *Statesmen*, 308; quoting Sykes, but not giving the page.

[23] John Nicholls, *Original Letters and Papers of State addressed to Oliver Cromwell ...* (London 1743), 40.

[24] *Ibid.*, 41. Cromwell at this time was in the North in Scotland.

[25] *Ibid.*, 84.

[26] *Ibid.*, 78. I have used here some of Vane's phrases out of context, but have, I believe, correctly expressed his attitudes.

[27] *Ibid.*, 79. Italics are mine.

[28] I can discover no contemporary letters, telling of his inner struggles, in his years of retirement.

[29] *Diary of Thomas Burton*, ed. J. T. Rutt, 4 vols. (London, 1828), III, 490. Note Vane's remarks in Parliament on Feb. 24, 1658/9. "I am not able ... to understand how the ... war with Spain, hath been agreeable at all to the interest of the state ... Our counsels have been mingled with France, and taken from the cardinal, who goeth upon the most tyrannical principles of government in the world."

[30] The Preface to the Reader is signed "From Belleau, April 20, 1655."

[31] I have used the edition printed in *The Somers Collection of Tracts,* ed. W. Scott (London, 1811), VI, 303–316.

[32] *A Needful Corrective* is a very rare tract. I have used the copy at the Bodleian and also the one at Yale. No publication date is given. Firth in the *Dictionary of National Biography* gives no date. Hosmer suggests Vane wrote this tract in 1657. It was published in London in 1660, according to Wing.

[33] In the British Museum copy, the title of the tract is *The Peoples Cause Stated.* Firth and Foster do not give the date, and Wing does not list it. Hosmer (p. 453) dates *The People's Case* in 1661, when Vane was in prison.

[34] *State Trials,* VI, 119–202.

[35] *Burton,* III and IV.

[36] *Ancient Foundations, The Valley of Jehoshaphat,* and *Concerning Government* are the three which I am convinced must be by Vane. The British Museum collection of tracts is G13817. In this collection are also: *A Letter from Sir H. V. to the Protector,* which can also be found in *State Trials,* V, 796–798 under a different heading; *A Letter of Sir H. V. to his Lady;* and several others not dealing with his political ideas, as for example, *of Friendship, of Enemies, upon Death.*

[37] Page 181. He also wrote in *The Retired Man's Meditations* that faith in Christ gives man "a raisedness of discerning and enlargedness of his natural mind." He becomes "a copartner and coheir with Christ" enabled "to do the will of God in earth as it is done in heaven" (75).

[38] *Ibid.,* 183.

[39] *Ibid.,* 384.

[40] *The People's Case,* 106.

[41] *The Retired Man's Meditations,* 183.

[42] *A Letter of Sir Henry Vane to his Lady, from the Isle of Scylly* (1662), 97.

[43] *The Retired Man's Meditations,* Preface to the Reader.

[44] *Ancient Foundations,* 120.

[45] There is no attempt in this essay to suggest or trace the sources of Vane's theology. Jacob Boehme may have been an earlier writer influencing him.

[46] *The Retired Man's Meditations,* 383.

[47] In most of his political writings, but particularly in *The Retired Man's Meditations* and *Ancient Foundations,* these ideas are put forth.

[48] *A Needful Corrective,* a2.

[49] Vane was not interested, as Harrington was, in the details of government.

[50] *The Retired Man's Meditations,* 387.

[51] *Ibid.*, 388. In his writings, and particularly in *The Retired Man's Meditations,* Vane regularly uses the phrase "outward man."

[52] *A Healing Question,* 306.

[53] *Ibid.*, 307. Apparently Vane believed that Anglicans, Catholics, Jews, and pagans should possess this spiritual freedom.

[54] See pages 47–49 of this article.

[55] *The Retired Man's Meditations,* 395.

[56] *A Healing Question,* 305.

[57] *A Needful Corrective,* 3, 4.

[58] *Ibid.*, 4.

[59] *The Retired Man's Meditations,* 385.

[60] *A Needful Corrective,* 3.

[61] Judges 20:11.

[62] *The Retired Man's Meditations,* 390.

[63] *Ibid.*, 395.

[64] *A Healing Question,* 310, 311.

[65] *A Needful Corrective,* 4.

[66] *Ibid.*, 3.

[67] *Ibid.*, 4. This government, however, was capable, he maintained in his trial, of developing into a right government. See pages 65–70.

[68] *The Retired Man's Meditations,* 389.

[69] *A Healing Question,* 311.

[70] *Ibid.*

[71] *A Needful Corrective,* 5.

[72] *Burton,* III, 171, 172.

[73] *Ibid.*, 176. See pages 52–54, where Vane's ideas, expressed in Parliament in 1659, are discussed more fully.

[74] *Ibid.*, 177.

[75] *A Healing Question,* 310. Since Vane was not concerned with the particular structure of right government, he never explains how the supremacy of an associated people actually operates.

[76] *Ibid.*, 308.

[77] *A Healing Question,* 311.

[78] *The People's Case,* 112.

[79] *Burton,* III, 227.

[80] *A Healing Question,* 310, 311. See also *The Retired Man's Meditations,* 388, where Vane states that the magistrate hath "the right of coercion" over the "outward man."

[81] *A Needful Corrective,* 3, 4.

[82] *The People's Case,* 110. Vane is referring here to a legislative act of king, lords, and commons.

[83] *The People's Case,* 98.

[84] Note, for example, the following statement, taken from Rousseau's *Social Contract:* "If the State is a moral person whose life is the union of its members, and if the most important of its cares is the care for its

own preservation, it must have a universal and compelling force, in order to move and dispose each part as may be most advantageous to the whole" (W. Y. Elliott and N. A. McDonald, *Western Political Heritage,* New York, 1949, 642).

[85] *Burton,* III, 172.

[86] Vane wrote Roger Williams, Feb. 8, 1653/4 asking him, Are there not "public minded self denying spirits, that at least, upon the grounds of public safety, equity, and prudence, can find out some way or means of union and reconciliation for you amongst yourselves?" (Hosmer, *op. cit.,* 424, quoting *Rhode Island Colonial Records,* I, 285).

[87] *The Retired Man's Meditations,* Preface to the Reader.

[88] *A Needful Corrective,* 5.

[89] *Ibid.,* 6.

[90] *Ibid.*

[91] *Ibid.,* 4.

[92] *A Healing Question,* 315.

[93] *Ibid.,* 304.

[94] *Ibid.*

[95] *Ibid.,* 307.

[96] *Ibid.*

[97] *Ibid.,* 312, 313.

[98] In his biography of Vane, Hosmer recognized (p. 444) the importance of Vane's proposal for a constitutional convention.

[99] *A Needful Corrective,* 6.

[100] *Ibid.,* 8. In *A Healing Question* (p. 312) Vane points out that if a right beginning is made, God will help to continue the good work.

[101] *A Needful Corrective,* 6.

[102] *Ibid.*

[103] In the following speeches I have quoted Vane literally whenever possible. At times, however, as indicated in the footnotes, I have summarized his remarks and at others have changed the order of his words in order to make the meaning of his remarks clearer, without giving the debate in detail.

[104] *Burton,* III, 180.

[105] *Ibid.,* 171.

[106] *Ibid.* The wording is my own.

[107] *Burton,* III, 176. These words are Vane's, taken from different paragraphs on p. 176.

[108] *Ibid.,* 177.

[109] *Ibid.,* 178.

[110] *Burton,* IV, 71.

[111] The wording is my own. See *Burton,* III, 337.

[112] *Burton,* III, 227.

[113] *Ibid.,* 492.

[114] *Burton,* IV, 180.

[115] *Ibid.,* 72.

[116] It is true that in his later writings there are occasional hints that Vane is despairing of achieving right government on earth. Only in heaven might it be possible.

[117] *A Needful Corrective,* 2.

[118] In his *Mysticism and Democracy in the English Commonwealth* (Cambridge, Mass., 1932), 117, Rufus Jones states that Vane was a friend of Peter Sterry, a mystic and also a Platonist, who for a time preached to the Council of State in the period of the Commonwealth.

[119] *Ancient Foundations, The Valley of Jehoshaphat.*

[120] *The People's Case,* 99, 100. The italicizing of Community and Society is my own.

[121] *Ibid.,* 102.

[122] *Ibid.,* 110.

[123] *Ibid.,* 101.

[124] *Ibid.,* 111.

[125] *State Trials,* VI, 194 and 196.

[126] *Ibid.,* 158. It should be noted that Vane quotes the king's answer to the Nineteen Propositions.

[127] M. Judson, *The Crisis of the Constitution* (New Brunswick, 1949), 396–407. There is no evidence I can discover that Vane was familiar with Hunton's writings.

[128] *State Trials,* VI, 153.

[129] *Ibid.,* 161.

[130] *The People's Case,* 104.

[131] *State Trials,* VI, 161. The italics are mine.

[132] *The People's Case,* 105, 106. In his trial he said (*State Trials,* VI, 160), "The politic capacity of the king hath properly no body nor soul, for it is formed by the policy of man."

[133] *The People's Case,* 103.

[134] *Ibid.*

[135] *A Healing Question,* 305. His contention that Parliament had acted correctly is interesting in relation to remarks he made in a brief tract, *Concerning Government.* This work looks to me like a common-place book, including statements (or summaries by Vane) of excerpts of Bodin, Calvin, etc. On page 124 Vane writes as follows, "But all con-trarient actings against the prince, are not to be accounted a resisting of the power, especially when the whole state is concerned, and the business is managed by public trustees, called and authorized by law, as conservers of the state; and defenders of the public liberties and laws thereof. In such a public capacity, to stand in the gap, when a breach is made, and hinder any change or attempt that would ruinate the state is duty."

[136] *The Parliamentary or Constitutional History of England* (1753), XVIII, 291.

87

[137] *Ibid.*

[138] *Burton,* III, 74. The quotation continues, "... out of my tenderness of blood. Yet, all power being thus in the people originally, I myself was afterward in the business."

[139] *State Trials,* VI, 164.

[140] *Burton,* III, 176.

[141] *Ancient Foundations,* 117.

[142] *Ibid.,* 118.

[143] *Ibid.,* 120.

[144] *The Retired Man's Meditations,* 393, 394. The italics are my own.

[145] In his biography of Vane, Sykes states (p. 9) that Vane did not set forth his principles for fear it would prevent him from "doing anything at all. He therefore for small matters, rather than nothing, went hand in hand with them step by step, their own pace as the pace of the times would permit."

[146] T. H. Green recognizes the importance of Vane and his utopian ideas. See his *Four Lectures on the English Commonwealth* in *Works of T. H. Green* (London, 1885–1911), V. III, 277–365.

[147] E. Clarendon, *The History of the Rebellion and Civil Wars in England,* ed. W. Macray, 6 vols. (Oxford, 1888), VI, 148.

[148] *Ibid.,* III, 217.

[149] *Ibid.,* I, 247.

[150] G. Davies, *The Restoration of Charles II* (San Marino, 1955), 145.

[151] One of the great enigmas concerning Vane's behavior upon which I cannot shed any light from my study of his political principles concerns his actions in the summer and fall of 1659. Although in all of his writings Vane insisted that force or military might must be subordinate to a properly associated people, he himself seemed at that time to look to the army as a means to advance the cause of right government. Did the end justify the means to him, as one suspects it did when the young Vane turned over to Pym the evidence against Strafford? His behavior in 1659 needs careful study in relation to his whole career.

[152] See letter to Cromwell given on pp. 75–77 of this article.

[153] I have used the copy of this letter, bound with other tracts of Vane in the British Museum's copy of *The People's Case,* G 13817 (5).

[154] *Ibid.,* 6–8.

[155] *A Healing Question,* 305, 306.

[156] *Ancient Foundations,* 121.

[157] Abbott, *Cromwell,* IV, 872.

[158] *Ibid.,* 470.